Introduction

Back-to-School Night is coming and you need a bulletin board idea. That's a perfect time to pull out *Portraits for Classroom Bulletin Boards*. Simply photocopy any or all of the fifteen portraits and biographies in this book—artists whose special talents and achievements have kept their names alive over the centuries.

Be creative to make an attractive display. You can create dramatic effects by copying the pages on brightly colored paper. Or, use white paper and mount the sheets on backgrounds of different colors.

Besides creating something that administrators, other teachers, and parents will admire, you can use the portraits to inspire your students as well. Display them throughout the year to bring to life these famous names from the pages of art history.

You can even turn these portraits into a research-writing activity. The biographies provided here are necessarily very limited; most suggest topics that could be the subject of further inquiry. Challenge your class to see what they can discover in the library about each of these artists and their life's work. Ask students to write their own paragraphs—then display their work alongside the appropriate portraits on your bulletin board.

You might also put together books to display your classes' research work. Give students copies of the smaller portraits found at the back of this book. These can be colored with markers and used as illustrations for the student reports. Collect the reports in binders for display at your open house. Teachers and parents alike will enjoy flipping through the books made by your different classes; students, too, will be interested in seeing each other's work.

With *Portraits for Classroom Bulletin Boards,* you get your students involved in creating graphically appealing bulletin boards. At the same time, you improve their cultural literacy by acquainting them with legendary names from the history of Western civilization.

Portraits are also available for mathematicians, scientists, authors, and poets.

Artists

Short biographies and portraits for the following artists appear in this book in chronological order.

Leonardo da Vinci (1452-1519)

Albrecht Dürer (1471-1528)

Michelangelo Buonarroti (1475-1564)

Raphael (1483-1520)

Rembrant van Rijn (1606-1669)

Francisco Goya (1746-1828)

Edgar Degas (1834-1917)

Winslow Homer (1836-1910)

Claude Monet (1840-1926)

Paul Gauguin (1848-1903)

Vincent van Gogh (1853-1890)

Toulouse-Lautrec (1864-1901)

Henri Matisse (1869-1954)

Pablo Picasso (1881-1973)

Salvador Dali (1904-1989)

Leonardo da Vinci (1452–1519), the greatest genius of the Italian Renaissance, was a man of many talents—a painter, sculptor, architect, engineer, scientist, musician, inventor, and writer.

Leonardo had a great desire to learn all he could about everything. His powers of scientific observation served him well as an artist; his work shows how much he understood about anatomy, proportion, and the structure and function of things. What he learned from nature, he applied to his many inventions, including helicopters, parachutes, gliders, and other flying machines. He recorded his ideas in voluminous notebooks filled with detailed sketches. His notes, written from right to left, can be read only in a mirror.

Founder of the classic style of painting of the High Renaissance, Leonardo was among the first to use the chiaroscuro technique. He completed very few paintings in his lifetime, but each one is considered a masterpiece. These include the unfinished *Adoration of the Magi* in Florence, the *Madonna of the Rocks,* and the *Last Supper,* a fresco painting in Milan that is now badly damaged. His *Mona Lisa* may be the most famous painting in the world.

Leonardo da Vinci

Albrecht Dürer (1471–1528) was a German painter and engraver. On travels to Venice, Dürer was greatly influenced by Italian Renaissance art. He took home many new ideas and skills, fusing the German and Italian methods of painting and becoming the leader of the German Renaissance school of painting.

Most famous for his engravings, Dürer produced a vast number of woodcuts and is regarded as the inventor of etching. His copperplate engravings include three masterpieces: *St. Jerome in his Study; Knight, Death and the Devil;* and *Melancolia.* Dürer's sensitive landscape and nature studies, characterized by realistic detail, also stand out as important works of art. With his pencil and watercolors, he captured the special textures of nature. Two good examples are *The Great Piece of Turf* and *The Hare.*

Dürer's many self-portraits reflect an amazing self-awareness, showing how he felt about himself at various stages of his life. He painted the first at age 13 and the last at 52, four years before his death. A collection of more than 100 of his works can be seen in the Albertina Museum in Vienna.

Albrecht Dürer

Michelangelo Buonarroti (1475-1564), painter, sculptor, and architect, was the most celebrated artist of the Italian Renaissance.

Michelangelo created exquisite marble sculptures, alive with strength and energy. His painting, too, resembles sculpture, each figure rendered with technical perfection and bursting with vitality. He was just 24 when he carved the *Pièta* that immediately brought him fame. His towering sculpture of *David* is a masterpiece of lifelike sculpturing.

His greatest achievement as a painter was the ceiling of the Sistine Chapel in Rome. This ceiling is 130 feet long, 43 feet wide, and curved like a half barrel. The fresco took four years to complete, and Michelangelo spent most of this time lying on his back on a scaffold 59 feet above the floor.

As he grew older, Michelangelo tired of painting and devoted his final years to architecture. He served as the chief architect for the magnificent domed St. Peter's Church, largest in the Christian world. During his lifetime Michelangelo also wrote many poems, mostly love sonnets, although he never married.

Michelangelo

Raphael (1483–1520) was a Renaissance painter and architect, sometimes called the "Prince of Italian painting." His real name was Raffaello Sanzio.

Raphael's early work in Florence included portraits of well-to-do citizens, which he drew in lifelike proportion, using soft, rich colors of paint with light and dark tones to make the figures look round and solid. His portraits caught the attention of Pope Julius II in Rome, who asked Raphael to paint frescos on the walls of the Vatican. These paintings include *The School of Athens,* 25 feet high and 40 feet long, painted in classic style. Raphael preceded Michelangelo as architect of St. Peter's Church, but little of his design was ever used.

Raphael is known for the unity and harmony of his compositions. He was an expert at creating graceful and idealized figures, as seen in his many gentle Madonnas. His *Sistine Madonna* is considered by some as the world's greatest painting. Raphael died suddenly at 37, but he had already assured his fame, along with Leonardo and Michelangelo, as one of the great trio of Renaissance art geniuses.

Raphael

Rembrant van Rijn (1606-1669) was the greatest of all Dutch painters. His work demonstrates the dramatic use of light and shadow (chiaroscuro) with rich colors and texture. Rembrandt's style had a great influence on the art of his day and, during the 18th and 19th centuries, was the model and inspiration of many painters.

Early in his career in Amsterdam, Rembrandt was a fashionable portrait painter. His elegant group portrait *Anatomy Lesson of Dr. Tulp* was highly regarded. He was also recognized for his mountainous landscapes and was considered a master of etching. Rembrandt painted nearly 100 self-portraits throughout his life. These reveal his growth as an artist, but also capture the discourage-ment he often felt because of personal troubles.

One of his most famous paintings, *The Night Watch,* marked a turning point in his life. For the first time he painted as he wanted to, and not to please others. Although his painting was a dramatic masterpiece, it was not the group portrait that his subjects had expected. His popularity declined, and he died in poverty. Today Rembrandt's paintings, drawings, and etchings are among the most valued museum possessions all over the world.

Rembrant van Rijn

Francisco Goya (1746–1828), a Spanish painter and lithograph artist, was the most important European painter of his era.

A series of tapestries for the Spanish royal court, masterpieces of rococo design, rank with his greatest achievements. Although he became a court painter, Goya sympathized with the goals of the French Revolution, not with the monarchy he served. His portraits of Spanish nobility, such as *Charles IV and His Family*, lay bare the viciousness and corruption of the aristocracy. Many of Goya's works reflect the bitter experiences of war. *The 3rd of May, 1808* realistically portrays the execution of a group of Madrid citizens, conveying man's inhumanity to man with great intensity and drama.

In his later years, Goya became interested in the new art of lithography. His series of bullfight scenes are among the greatest lithographs ever made. Although Goya was recognized outside Spain only after his death, his highly original approach to art had a profound influence on 19th and 20th century painting.

Francisco Goya

Edgar Degas (1834–1917) was a French painter and sculptor who worked with the impressionists.

Unlike the other impressionist painters, Degas loathed painting outdoors. He was not concerned with spontaneity and was more interested in movement than in color. He did, however, share their interest in painting scenes from everyday life, taking as his subjects working women, street cafes, the horse races, and ballet dancers.

An admirer of Japanese prints with their asymmetrical balance, Degas disregarded the classical rules of composition. His carefully planned works feature unusual angles and off-center subjects. His sculptures of dancers and horses, as well as his paintings, exhibit a beauty of line and great mastery of movement. A superb draftsman, Degas invented new ways to use pastels, applying colors in many soft and powdery layers. This technique was especially effective in his ballet scenes.

In his lifetime, Degas sold only one work, *The Cotton Exchange at New Orleans,* but today his paintings and sketches sell for astonishing prices.

Edgar Degas

Winslow Homer (1836–1910) was one of the most powerful and original American painters of the 19th century.

After working in a lithographer's office, where he learned to make prints from original drawings, Homer became an illustrator for *Harper's Weekly.* When he served as Civil War correspondent for this periodical, his once happy scenes of everyday life turned to somber illustrations that showed the agony of the battlefield.

Later Homer gave up illustration and devoted himself to painting, taking as his subjects the woodsmen of the forest and the fishermen of the sea. His careful use of color, light, and shadow in his oils and watercolors add to the unsurpassed realism of his work.

Toward the end of his life, Homer settled in a small cabin on the rocky coast of Maine. He concentrated on painting the sea and its many moods, capturing its intense, bright atmosphere with simple washes of vivid color. He loved to paint dramatic, stormy seas, and his seascapes are considered his finest pictures. These include *Breezing Up*, *Fog Warning*, *The Gulf Stream,* and *Northeaster.*

Raphael

Rembrant van Rijn (1606-1669) was the greatest of all Dutch painters. His work demonstrates the dramatic use of light and shadow (chiaroscuro) with rich colors and texture. Rembrandt's style had a great influence on the art of his day and, during the 18th and 19th centuries, was the model and inspiration of many painters.

Early in his career in Amsterdam, Rembrandt was a fashionable portrait painter. His elegant group portrait *Anatomy Lesson of Dr. Tulp* was highly regarded. He was also recognized for his mountainous landscapes and was considered a master of etching. Rembrandt painted nearly 100 self-portraits throughout his life. These reveal his growth as an artist, but also capture the discourage-ment he often felt because of personal troubles.

One of his most famous paintings, *The Night Watch,* marked a turning point in his life. For the first time he painted as he wanted to, and not to please others. Although his painting was a dramatic masterpiece, it was not the group portrait that his subjects had expected. His popularity declined, and he died in poverty. Today Rembrandt's paintings, drawings, and etchings are among the most valued museum possessions all over the world.

Rembrant van Rijn

Francisco Goya (1746–1828), a Spanish painter and lithograph artist, was the most important European painter of his era.

A series of tapestries for the Spanish royal court, masterpieces of rococo design, rank with his greatest achievements. Although he became a court painter, Goya sympathized with the goals of the French Revolution, not with the monarchy he served. His portraits of Spanish nobility, such as *Charles IV and His Family*, lay bare the viciousness and corruption of the aristocracy. Many of Goya's works reflect the bitter experiences of war. *The 3rd of May, 1808* realistically portrays the execution of a group of Madrid citizens, conveying man's inhumanity to man with great intensity and drama.

In his later years, Goya became interested in the new art of lithography. His series of bullfight scenes are among the greatest lithographs ever made. Although Goya was recognized outside Spain only after his death, his highly original approach to art had a profound influence on 19th and 20th century painting.

Francisco Goya

Edgar Degas (1834–1917) was a French painter and sculptor who worked with the impressionists.

Unlike the other impressionist painters, Degas loathed painting outdoors. He was not concerned with spontaneity and was more interested in movement than in color. He did, however, share their interest in painting scenes from everyday life, taking as his subjects working women, street cafes, the horse races, and ballet dancers.

An admirer of Japanese prints with their asymmetrical balance, Degas disregarded the classical rules of composition. His carefully planned works feature unusual angles and off-center subjects. His sculptures of dancers and horses, as well as his paintings, exhibit a beauty of line and great mastery of movement. A superb draftsman, Degas invented new ways to use pastels, applying colors in many soft and powdery layers. This technique was especially effective in his ballet scenes.

In his lifetime, Degas sold only one work, *The Cotton Exchange at New Orleans,* but today his paintings and sketches sell for astonishing prices.

Edgar Degas

Winslow Homer (1836–1910) was one of the most powerful and original American painters of the 19th century.

After working in a lithographer's office, where he learned to make prints from original drawings, Homer became an illustrator for *Harper's Weekly*. When he served as Civil War correspondent for this periodical, his once happy scenes of everyday life turned to somber illustrations that showed the agony of the battlefield.

Later Homer gave up illustration and devoted himself to painting, taking as his subjects the woodsmen of the forest and the fishermen of the sea. His careful use of color, light, and shadow in his oils and watercolors add to the unsurpassed realism of his work.

Toward the end of his life, Homer settled in a small cabin on the rocky coast of Maine. He concentrated on painting the sea and its many moods, capturing its intense, bright atmosphere with simple washes of vivid color. He loved to paint dramatic, stormy seas, and his seascapes are considered his finest pictures. These include *Breezing Up*, *Fog Warning*, *The Gulf Stream*, and *Northeaster*.

Winslow Homer

Claude Monet (1840–1926), a French landscape painter, was a leader of the impressionist movement. In fact, Monet's painting *Sunrise, an Impression* was the source of the term "impressionism." He worked closely with Manet, Pissaro, and Renoir, each having a great influence on the others.

Monet always worked out of doors, using small touches of unmixed color to show how light was reflected from water and leaves. He liked to paint in the full midday sun to avoid shadows. His technique was based on the idea that nothing has a single, fixed color; rather, the color changes according to the way the light strikes it at any given moment.

Monet's fascination with light led him to paint several studies of exactly the same view—haystacks, for example, or garden scenes—at different hours and in different seasons to show the varying effects of sunlight on a subject. His "series paintings" include the famous *Rouen Cathedral* and his lyrical *Water Lilies*. Monet's paintings, with their emphasis on light and color, had a great influence on later abstract painters.

Claude Monet

Paul Gauguin (1848–1903) was an important French post-impressionistic painter. Once a prosperous stockbroker in Paris, Gauguin began painting as a hobby. At 35 he abandoned his career to devote himself to painting. Along with van Gogh and Cezanne, he founded a new art movement called symbolism.

Gauguin rejected European civilization, which he saw as dedicated to material wealth at the expense of the human spirit. For a time he lived among the peasants in western France where religion was still a vital part of life. He depicted their simple faith in *The Yellow Christ* and *Offerings of Gratitude*.

A few years later, Gauguin sailed to Tahiti where he did some of his finest work. His paintings of the natives and the lush tropics of the South Seas are primitive and exotic. They feature abstract patterns, strong contours, and bright, flat, non-naturalistic colors. Gauguin produced many lithographs and fine woodcuts in the same primitive style.

After a brief return to France, where his paintings did not sell, Gauguin died in poverty and despair in the South Seas, unaware of his profound influence on the art of the 20th century.

Paul Gauguin

Vincent van Gogh (1853–1890) was a Dutch post-impressionist painter whose intense, emotional pictures are well-known throughout the world.

Encouraged to become an art dealer like his brother, van Gogh went to Paris where his brother introduced him to the impressionists. Van Gogh loved art, but he was not a businessman. He soon moved to Arles to pursue his own career as a painter. One of the first to use the expressive value of color, van Gogh developed a highly personal style, which featured the impasto technique of applying color in broad masses with vigorous brushstrokes. His style was a precursor of modern expressionism, which strives to communicate the inner feelings of the artist rather than visual reality.

Van Gogh painted many masterpieces during his short lifetime, including *Starry Night, Sunflowers, Iris, The Postman Roulin, L'Arlesienne,* and *Self-Portrait with Bandaged Ear.*

Beset with mental illness, van Gogh cut off his own ear in an argument with Gauguin. He voluntarily entered an asylum and, at 37, shot himself. Although his paintings sell today for as much as $50 million, he died a very poor man.

Vincent van Gogh

Henri de Toulouse-Lautrec (1864–1901) was a French painter and lithograph artist, best known for his decorative theater and dance hall posters.

Born an aristocrat, Toulouse-Lautrec was a sickly child, physically deformed by an accident that stunted his growth. He started painting at an early age and soon made friends with Manet, Degas, Gauguin, and van Gogh. He loved the night life of the Montmartre district of Paris. The music halls, the night clubs, the theater, the circuses all provided subjects for his painting.

Toulouse-Lautrec disliked posed models, preferring to capture his subjects in action. His paintings began as swift sketches, each catching a precise moment in time with a series of quick lines. Later he would develop his sketches into paintings, using vivid color to create a strong graphic effect. Despite the decorative nature of his work, it also reveals a deep understanding of the people he portrayed. His lithograph *At the Moulin Rouge* mercilessy reveals the character of performers and customers in a nightclub scene.

Since Toulouse-Lautrec's early death at 37, his posters and lithographs have become very popular.

Winslow Homer

Claude Monet (1840–1926), a French landscape painter, was a leader of the impressionist movement. In fact, Monet's painting *Sunrise, an Impression* was the source of the term "impressionism." He worked closely with Manet, Pissaro, and Renoir, each having a great influence on the others.

Monet always worked out of doors, using small touches of unmixed color to show how light was reflected from water and leaves. He liked to paint in the full midday sun to avoid shadows. His technique was based on the idea that nothing has a single, fixed color; rather, the color changes according to the way the light strikes it at any given moment.

Monet's fascination with light led him to paint several studies of exactly the same view— haystacks, for example, or garden scenes—at different hours and in different seasons to show the varying effects of sunlight on a subject. His "series paintings" include the famous *Rouen Cathedral* and his lyrical *Water Lilies*. Monet's paintings, with their emphasis on light and color, had a great influence on later abstract painters.

Claude Monet

Paul Gauguin (1848–1903) was an important French post-impressionistic painter. Once a prosperous stockbroker in Paris, Gauguin began painting as a hobby. At 35 he abandoned his career to devote himself to painting. Along with van Gogh and Cezanne, he founded a new art movement called symbolism.

Gauguin rejected European civilization, which he saw as dedicated to material wealth at the expense of the human spirit. For a time he lived among the peasants in western France where religion was still a vital part of life. He depicted their simple faith in *The Yellow Christ* and *Offerings of Gratitude*.

A few years later, Gauguin sailed to Tahiti where he did some of his finest work. His paintings of the natives and the lush tropics of the South Seas are primitive and exotic. They feature abstract patterns, strong contours, and bright, flat, non-naturalistic colors. Gauguin produced many lithographs and fine woodcuts in the same primitive style.

After a brief return to France, where his paintings did not sell, Gauguin died in poverty and despair in the South Seas, unaware of his profound influence on the art of the 20th century.

Paul Gauguin

Vincent van Gogh (1853–1890) was a Dutch post-impressionist painter whose intense, emotional pictures are well-known throughout the world.

Encouraged to become an art dealer like his brother, van Gogh went to Paris where his brother introduced him to the impressionists. Van Gogh loved art, but he was not a businessman. He soon moved to Arles to pursue his own career as a painter. One of the first to use the expressive value of color, van Gogh developed a highly personal style, which featured the impasto technique of applying color in broad masses with vigorous brushstrokes. His style was a precursor of modern expressionism, which strives to communicate the inner feelings of the artist rather than visual reality.

Van Gogh painted many masterpieces during his short lifetime, including *Starry Night, Sunflowers, Iris, The Postman Roulin, L'Arlesienne,* and *Self-Portrait with Bandaged Ear.*

Beset with mental illness, van Gogh cut off his own ear in an argument with Gauguin. He voluntarily entered an asylum and, at 37, shot himself. Although his paintings sell today for as much as $50 million, he died a very poor man.

Vincent van Gogh

Henri de Toulouse-Lautrec (1864–1901) was a French painter and lithograph artist, best known for his decorative theater and dance hall posters.

Born an aristocrat, Toulouse-Lautrec was a sickly child, physically deformed by an accident that stunted his growth. He started painting at an early age and soon made friends with Manet, Degas, Gauguin, and van Gogh. He loved the night life of the Montmartre district of Paris. The music halls, the night clubs, the theater, the circuses all provided subjects for his painting.

Toulouse-Lautrec disliked posed models, preferring to capture his subjects in action. His paintings began as swift sketches, each catching a precise moment in time with a series of quick lines. Later he would develop his sketches into paintings, using vivid color to create a strong graphic effect. Despite the decorative nature of his work, it also reveals a deep understanding of the people he portrayed. His lithograph *At the Moulin Rouge* mercilessy reveals the character of performers and customers in a nightclub scene.

Since Toulouse-Lautrec's early death at 37, his posters and lithographs have become very popular.

Toulouse-Lautrec

Henri Matisse (1869–1954), a French painter and sculptor, is considered one of the founding fathers of modern art.

Influenced by the impressionists, Matisse also incorporated elements from Persian art, medieval stained glass, and children's art into his own decorative style. He was the acknowledged leader of a group of expressionist painters, dubbed *les Fauves* (wild beasts) by art critics who were shocked by their radical approach to painting.

Matisse was enchanted by pure color and graceful lines. He strove to create a harmony of color and shape without losing the quality of either, combining bold contours and rhythmic outlines with broad sweeps of rich color. Matisse's work is also distinguished by its careful balance, simplicity of design, and masterful use of pattern. His favorite subjects were still lifes and interiors with women, but he used no shading and made no attempt to keep them true to life.

Matisse continued to develop his innovative style even into his last years, when he used scissors to cut bold, exciting designs from colored paper, as in his famous *Jazz* series.

Henri Matisse

Pablo Picasso (1881-1973), Spanish painter and sculptor, was the most influential artist of the 20th century. He was a founder of the abstract movement and, with his friend Georges Braque, originated cubism.

During Picasso's early years in Paris, he painted with mostly blue and rose tones as he studied line, shape, and value. With his *Les Demoiselles d'Avignon,* Picasso started an artistic revolution. In this painting, the figures are angular, distorted, and have been flattened into planes of color. This work contains all the elements of cubism, which simplifies the shapes of nature into geometric forms and distorts perspective, showing more than one view of an object at once. Picasso also developed the new medium of collage. His greatest work, *Guernica,* depicts the agony and horrors of war in a powerful style that draws from cubism but approaches surrealism.

A prolific artist for all of his 91 years, Picasso continually explored daring and unpredictable new directions in art. He did brilliant work in sculpture and every form of graphic arts, as well as ceramics, mosaics, and stage design. His works appear in museums and private collections all over the world.

Pablo Picasso

Salvador Dali (1904–1989), a Spanish painter, was the foremost figure of the surrealist movement in modern art. His work draws from the images and symbols of dreams, hallucinations, and the subconscious mind. While his paintings appear irrational, the startling juxtaposition of images works to reveal secrets of the human soul.

Dali's most famous painting, *The Persistence of Memory,* shows a desolate landscape with ordinary pocket watches that are limp and melting over cliffs and dead trees. Each detail is drawn with precise realism, creating a powerful, dreamlike effect.

After moving to the United States in 1940, Dali illustrated and wrote books, designed art films and sets for the ballet, and made surrealistic jewelry, ceramics, fabrics, furniture, and small sculptures. His books include two autobiographies, *The Secret Life of Salvador Dali* and *Diary of a Genius.*

Dali was very theatrical, flamboyant in his appearance, and loved publicity. Many critics consider him an artistic prankster; nonetheless, his works have secured him a place in the history of modern art.

Salvador Dali

Leonardo da Vinci

Albrecht Dürer

Michelangelo

Raphael

Rembrant van Rijn

Francisco Goya

Edgar Degas

Winslow Homer

Claude Monet

Paul Gauguin

Vincent van Gogh

Toulouse-Lautrec

Henri Matisse

Pablo Picasso

Salvador Dali